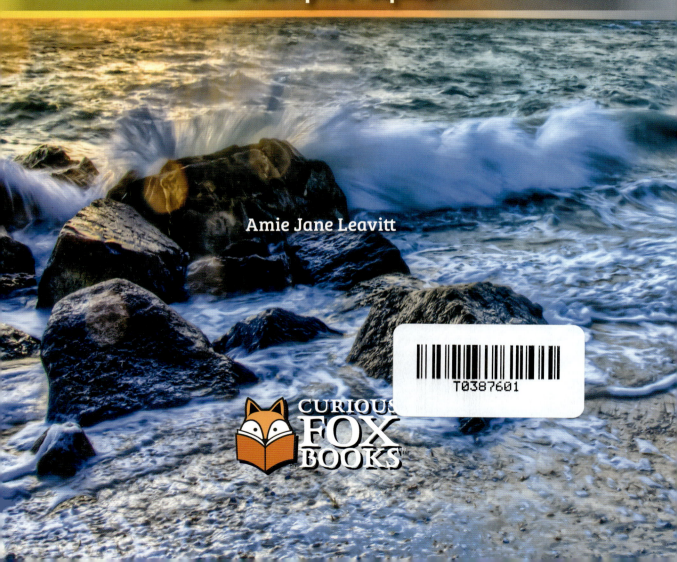

AMAZING CREATURES OF THE Gulf of Mexico

Learn About Animals Including Manatees, Seahorses, Hammerhead Sharks, and Vampire Squids!

Amie Jane Leavitt

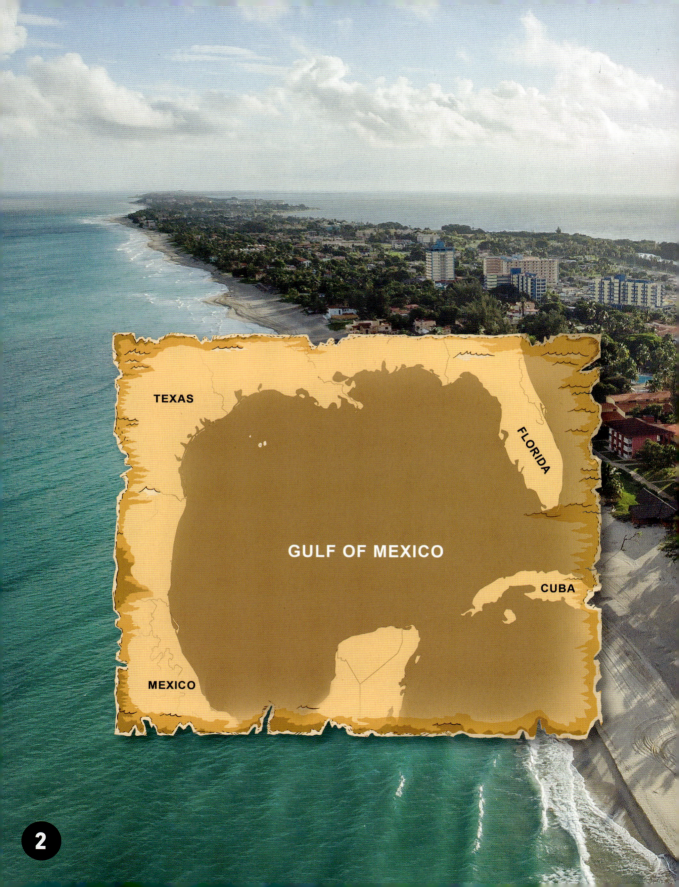

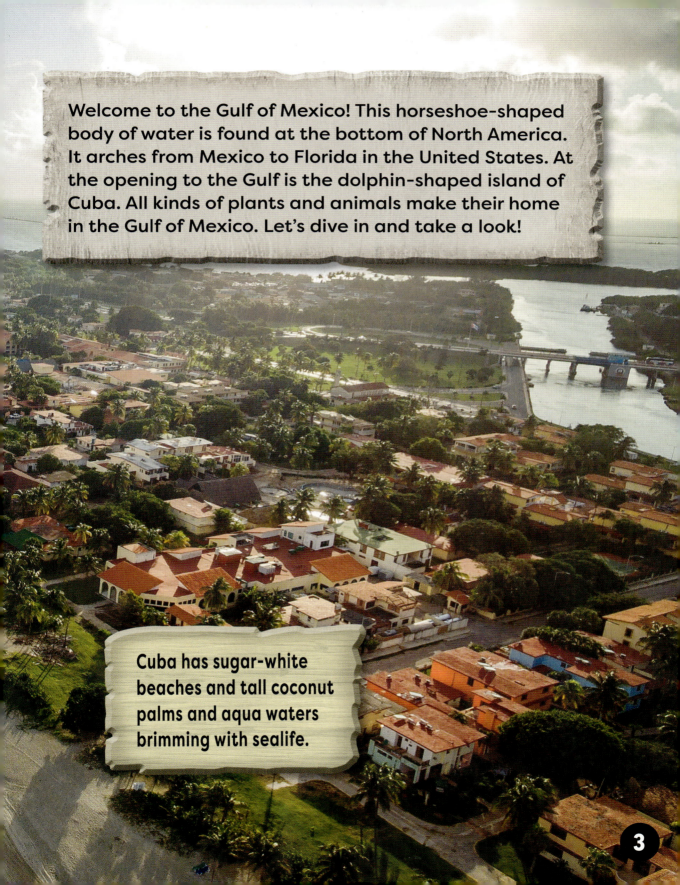

Welcome to the Gulf of Mexico! This horseshoe-shaped body of water is found at the bottom of North America. It arches from Mexico to Florida in the United States. At the opening to the Gulf is the dolphin-shaped island of Cuba. All kinds of plants and animals make their home in the Gulf of Mexico. Let's dive in and take a look!

Cuba has sugar-white beaches and tall coconut palms and aqua waters brimming with sealife.

Thirty-three major rivers drain into the Gulf of Mexico, including the Mississippi River. Where a river enters the Gulf, fresh river water mixes with salt water. River mud settles to create swampy areas called deltas (DEL-tuhs).

The American alligator is right at home in the warm delta. These animals lounge in the sun or lurk in the water, waiting to catch a meal. They are the largest alligators in the world, sometimes growing to over 14 feet (4.3 meters) long and weighing up to 1,000 pounds (453.6 kilograms).

Baby American alligators, known as "hatchlings," hatch from eggs and are born with yellow stripes. The mothers then move their babies to the water in their mouths. Alligator mothers care of their babies for one to two years.

The diamondback terrapin (a type of turtle) is another reptile that loves warm river deltas. They only climb onto the land to lay their eggs in nests on the sand. They spend most of the rest of their time in the water, catching fish, shrimp, snails, and other small creatures. They usually live to around 25 years old, but they can live up to 40 years!

Diamondback terrapins have large webbed feet that help them swim. Every terrapin's shell pattern and color is different, kind of like human fingerprints!

Seagrass grows in shallow waters along the coastlines. These plants grow blade-like leaves. Their roots help keep sand from washing away. The plants also help keep the water clear. Many types of sea animals live among these grasses.

The sea robin is a fish that lives in seagrass on the seafloor. It has spikes on its fins that act like legs. With these special fins, it can both swim and walk.

The sea hare is a soft-bodied animal, sometimes known as a sea slug, that also lives in the seagrass. Scientists named this creature the sea hare because of the long, thin "ears" that grow from its neck. These are organs called "rhinopores" that help the sea hare smell and taste.

Brown pelicans live along the coastlines. They dive down into the water and use their big pouched bills to scoop up fish. Brown pelicans are the smallest type of pelican, but they're still large seabirds. They can reach up to 5 feet (1.5 meters) tall and their wingspans can be up to 7½ feet (2.3 meters).

Brown pelicans prefer to fly low over coastal waters to spot fish. They usually avoid flying out over deep ocean waters.

Manatees have nostrils on top of their snouts that close tightly when they are swimming under the water. They usually come up for air every five minutes, opening their nostrils to breathe.

Manatees (MAN-uh-tees) live along the coasts of the Gulf of Mexico. These large mammals swim in shallow, slow-moving waters. Manatees eat underwater grasses, mangrove leaves, and algae (AL-jee). They can eat up to 200 pounds (90.7 kilograms) of food every day.

Manatees usually grow to be 10 feet (3.1 meters) long and weigh 1,200 pounds (544.3 kilograms). Manatees are also called "sea cows," but they're not related to cows at all. Their closest relative is actually the elephant!

Sargassum (sar-GAS-um) is a type of golden-brown seaweed. It floats in huge, thick mats on the water. The Gulf of Mexico has more sargassum than most of the earth's oceans.

Some fish live their whole lives in the sargassum. The sargassum fish is a type of frogfish that does just that. Its frilly fins act as camouflage (KAM-uh-flah-shh) to help it blend in with the seaweed and hide. It can also change its color a bit and hop on top of the seaweed if it needs to.

Female fish lay their eggs in sargassum mats. When the eggs hatch, the thick seaweed gives small fish a place to hide.

Sargassum is like a floating jungle. Crabs, seahorses, shrimp, tunas, billfish like marlins and sailfish, and other animals all live in or around sargassum mats. The larger fish rely on these mini jungles for food. Younger tunas will even hide from seabirds in the sargassum.

Seahorses often swim with a partner, linking their tails together. They also use their tails to hold onto seaweed while resting.

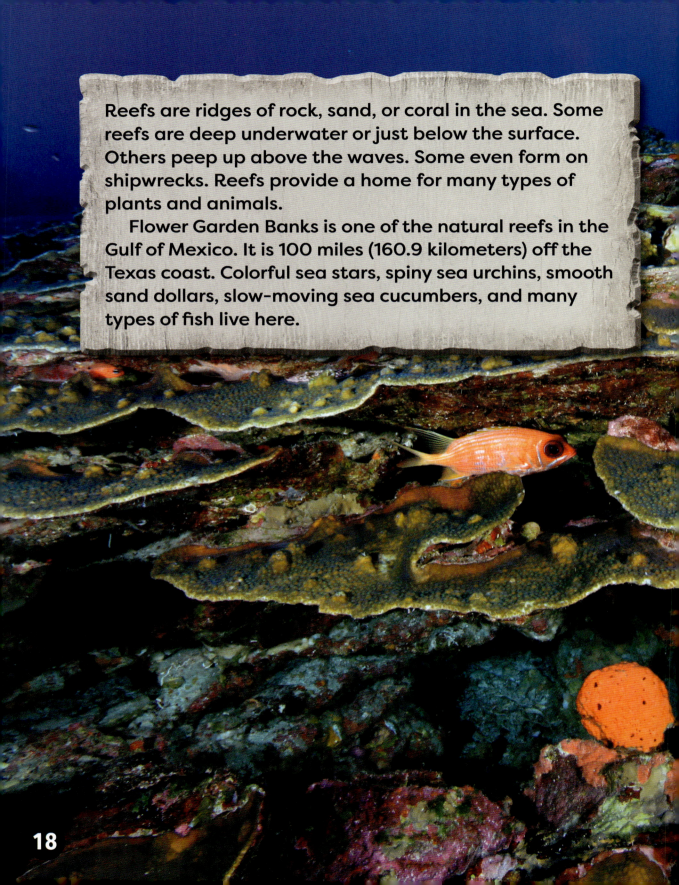

Reefs are ridges of rock, sand, or coral in the sea. Some reefs are deep underwater or just below the surface. Others peep up above the waves. Some even form on shipwrecks. Reefs provide a home for many types of plants and animals.

Flower Garden Banks is one of the natural reefs in the Gulf of Mexico. It is 100 miles (160.9 kilometers) off the Texas coast. Colorful sea stars, spiny sea urchins, smooth sand dollars, slow-moving sea cucumbers, and many types of fish live here.

Some sealife, like the long-spined urchin, have spiky (**SPY-kee**) bodies. The spikes help protect them from being eaten.

Many types of sharks and rays live and hunt in coral reefs. One of the most unusual sharks you'll see in Gulf reefs is the hammerhead shark. These huge fish can grow up to 20 feet (6.1 meters) long and weigh over 1,000 pounds (453.6 kilograms). Hammerheads are a little different from other sharks—they swim together in large schools during the day.

Because the hammerhead has its eyes on the ends of its T-shaped head, it can see everything above and below it.

The bottlenose dolphin can live for over 40 years. They're very smart and playful.

At least nine different types of dolphins live in the Gulf of Mexico. There are more Atlantic bottlenose dolphins here than in any other sea. These dolphins are light gray with a pinkish-white belly. They have a short nose and a full smile, with 80 to 100 teeth. They eat fish, squid, shrimp, crabs, and lobsters.

Groups of dolphins are called pods. Living in large groups helps keep dolphins safe from predators (PREH-dih-turs).

They can be rare to see, but many types of whales live in the Gulf of Mexico, including pilot whales, humpback whales, killer whales, and sperm whales.

Sperm whales can be up to 65 feet (19.8 meters) long and weigh about 50 tons (45.4 metric tons). They eat mainly squid that live on the seafloor—about 1 ton (0.9 metric ton) of squid every day! Sperm whales dive up to 3,000 feet (914.4 meters) deep for food.

The sperm whale has a huge brain—it's six times larger than a human brain. In fact, the sperm whale's brain is the largest brain of any animal that has ever lived.

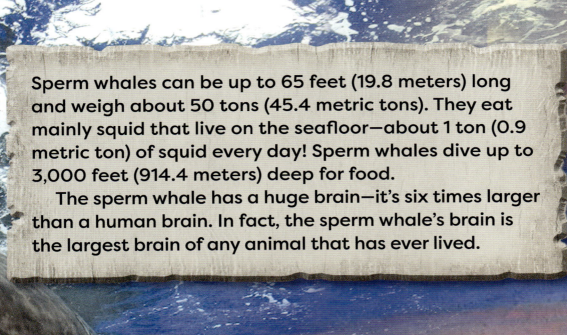

Rice's whale is also known as the Gulf of Mexico whale because it is only found in these waters. Scientists estimate that there are only around 50 Rice's whales in the world.

It is dark and cold in the deepest part of the Gulf of Mexico. Very little sunlight can reach this part of the sea. As a result, many unusual creatures dwell in this murky place. The vampire squid is one of them. This animal isn't really a squid, it just looks like one. It has huge blue eyes that help it see in the dark. It has eight arms connected by a web, and it can turn itself inside out for protection.

Some people call these star-shaped creatures "starfish." But they're really not fish at all, so they should be called "sea stars."

Some deep-sea dwellers are like fireflies. They glow in the dark in bright pink, yellow, purple, green, and blue. The glowing light helps these creatures find food and mates. Deep-sea fish, jellyfish, algae, bacteria (bak-TEER-ee-uh), worms, sea stars, and some kinds of sharks can all make their own light.

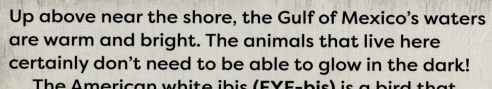

Up above near the shore, the Gulf of Mexico's waters are warm and bright. The animals that live here certainly don't need to be able to glow in the dark!

The American white ibis (EYE-bis) is a bird that spends its days in the gulf's shallow waters. It uses its long pointed beak to dig down into the mud and snatch all kinds of food from its wetland home. It eats fish, insects, reptiles, crabs, and even some kinds of plants.

Whether it's the shallow waters or the deep sea, there are many amazing creatures that call the Gulf of Mexico their home sweet home.

The roseate spoonbill is another bird with an odd beak that loves the warm areas on the coasts of the Gulf of Mexico. The spoon-shaped bill lets it sift through mud for food. These birds are pink because of the foods they eat.

FURTHER READING

Books

Hanes, Kathleen. *Seagrass Dreams: A Counting Book.* Lake Forest, CA: Seagrass Press, 2017.

Hoyt, Erich. *Creatures of the Deep.* Buffalo, NY: Firefly Ebooks, 2014.

Marsh, Laura. *National Geographic Readers: Manatees.* Washington, D.C.: National Geographic Children's books, 2014.

Marsh, Laura. *National Geographic Readers: Sea Turtles.* Washington, D.C.: National Geographic Society, 2011.

Marsh, Laura. *National Geographic Readers: Whales.* Washington, D.C.: National Geographic Society, 2011.

Priddy, Roger. *Smart Kids: Coral Reef.* London: Priddy Books, 2014.

Stewart, Melissa. *Dolphins.* Washington, D.C.: National Geographic Children's Books, 2011.

Web Sites

The Dolphin Research Center: "Manatee Facts for Kids"
https://www.dolphins.org/kids_manatee_facts

The Florida Museum of Natural History: "Life in Seagrasses"
https://www.floridamuseum.ufl.edu/southflorida/habitats/seagrasses/life/

GLOSSARY

algae (AL-jee)—Small plants that grow in the water.

bacteria (bak-TEER-ee-uh)—Very small living things that are made of only one cell.

camouflage (KAM-uh-flahshh)—A way for animals to blend into their surroundings to disguise and defend themselves against predators.

delta (DEL-tuh)—A swampy area shaped like a triangle that is formed when a river splits into smaller rivers before it flows into an ocean.

ibis (EYE-bis)—A type of wading bird with a long, down-curved beak used to dig for food.

manatees (MAN-uh-tees)—Large aquatic animals that live in shallow, slow-moving waters.

oasis (oh-AY-sis)—A place that provides peace and safety.

predators (PREH-dih-turs)—An animal that hunts other animals for food.

sargassum (sar-GAS-um)—A golden-brown seaweed that usually floats in large, thick mats on the water.

spiky (SPY-kee)—Having large, pointed spines to protect from predators.

squid (SKWID)—A deep-sea animal that has eight legs plus two longer arms; it can squirt ink to avoid enemies.

PHOTO CREDITS

p. 1—Chris McClanahan; pp. 2–3—Shutterstock/DTS Producciones; pp. 4–5—Shutterstock/Pierre Jean Durieu; p. 5 (inset)—Shutterstock/BlueBarronPhoto; pp. 6–7—Shutterstock/Jay Ondreicka; p. 7 (inset)—Shutterstock/Jeremy Laratro; pp. 8–9—Shutterstock/divedog; p. 8 (inset)—Shutterstock/dlearyous photography; p. 9 (inset)—Shutterstock/Jesus Cobaleda; pp.10–11—Shutterstock/William A. Morgan; p. 11 (inset)—Shutterstock/Alexey Stiop; pp.12–13—Shutterstock/Harry Collins Photography; p. 13 (inset)—Shutterstock/Andreas Vogel; pp. 14–15—Shutterstock/Ethan Daniels; p. 15 (inset)—Shutterstock/Eric Lemar; pp. 16–17—Shutterstock/Rich Carey; p. 17 (inset)—Shutterstock/Brent Barnes; pp. 18–19—Shutterstock/lego 19861111; pp. 20–21—Shutterstock/frantisekhojdysz; p. 21 (inset)—Shutterstock/Martin Prochazkacz; pp. 22–23—Shutterstock/Willyam Bradberry; p. 23 (inset)—Shutterstock/Andriy Nekrasov; pp. 28–29—Shutterstock/Martin Pelanek; p. 29 (inset)—Shutterstock/Carolyn Bartlett; All other photos—Public Domain.

INDEX

Algae 13, 27
American alligators 4–5
American white ibis 28–29
Bacteria 27
Bottlenose dolphins 22–23
Brown pelicans 10–11
Coral 18
Cuba 2, 3
Delta 4
Dolphins 3, 22–23
Fireflies 27
Florida 2, 3
Flower Garden Banks 18
Hammerhead sharks 20–21

Jellyfish 27
Long-spined urchin 19
Manatees 12–13
Mexico 2, 3
Mississippi River 4
Predator 23
Reefs 18–19
Rice's whales 25
Roseate spoonbill 29
Sargassum 14–16
Sargassum fish 15
Sea hare 9
Sea robin, 8
Sea stars 27

Seagrass 8–9
Seahorses 17
Sharks 20–21, 27
Sperm whales 24–25
Squid 22, 25, 26
Texas 2, 18
Turtles (diamondback
    terrapin) 6–7
United States 3
Vampire squid 26
Whales 24–25
Worms 27

© 2025 by Curious Fox Books™, an imprint of Fox Chapel Publishing Company, Inc.

Amazing Creatures of the Gulf of Mexico is a revision of *Water Planet: Life in the Gulf of Mexico*, originally published in 2018 by Purple Toad Publishing, Inc. Reproduction of its contents is strictly prohibited without written permission from the rights holder.

Paperback ISBN 979-8-89094-168-8
Hardcover ISBN 979-8-89094-169-5

Library of Congress Control Number: 2024950035

To learn more about the other great books from Fox Chapel Publishing, or to find a retailer near you, call toll-free at 800-457-9112 or visit us at *www.FoxChapelPublishing.com*.
You can also send mail to:
Fox Chapel Publishing
903 Square Street
Mount Joy, PA 17552

We are always looking for talented authors. To submit an idea, please send a brief inquiry to acquisitions@foxchapelpublishing.com.

Fox Chapel Publishing makes every effort to use environmentally friendly paper for printing.

Printed in China